GREAT AFRICAN AMERICANS IN

Literature

PAT REDIGER

Crabtree Publishing Company

Dedication

This series is dedicated to the African-American men and women who dared to follow their dreams. With courage, faith, and hard work, they overcame obstacles in their lives and went on to excel in their fields. They fought for civil rights and encouraged hope and self-reliance. They celebrated the glory of the athlete and the joy of knowledge and learning. They brought entertainment, poetry, and song to the world, and we are richer for it. *Outstanding African Americans* is both an acknowledgement of and a tribute to these people.

Project Manager
Amanda Woodrow

Writing Team
Karen Dudley
Pat Rediger

Editor
Virginia Mainprize

Research
Karen Dudley

Design and layout
Warren Clark
Karen Dudley

Photograph Credits
Archive Photos: pages 7 (Consolidated News), 10 (Camera Press), 27, 40 (Frank Capri/SAGA), 61; **Photograph by Miriam Berkley:** pages 46, 49; **Reuters/Bettman:** page 15; **UPI/Bettman:** pages 5, 13, 16, 38; **Blackstar:** pages 4, 6, 8 (Stratford), 11, 12 (Shapiro), 14 (Baer), 22 (Hawthorne); **Canapress Photo Service:** pages 18, 21, 23, 31, 37, 43; **Dial Books:** page 58 (Ackerman); **McDowell Colony:** page 42 (Bernice Perry); **Schomburg Center for Research in Black Culture, The New York Public Library, Astor, Lenox and Tilden Foundations:** pages 26, 28, 29, 30, 32; **Photograph by Layle Silbert:** pages 35, 55; **Urban Archives, Temple University:** pages 9, 25, 52; **Alice Walker:** pages 41, 44, 45; **Woodfin Camp & Associates:** pages 17, 20, 34, 36, 39 (Gotfryd).

Published by
Crabtree Publishing Company

350 Fifth Avenue,	360 York Road, R.R. 4	73 Lime Walk
Suite 3308	Niagara-on-the-Lake,	Headington
New York, New York	Ontario Canada	Oxford Ox3 7AD
U.S.A. 10018	L0S 1J0	United Kingdom

Cataloging-in-Publication Data

Rediger, Pat, 1966
   Great African Americans in literature/by Pat Rediger.
     p. cm. — (Outstanding African Americans series)
   Includes index.
   Summary: Profiles notable African Americans in the field of literature, including Maya Angelou, James Baldwin, and Mildred Taylor.
   ISBN 0-86505-802-4 (lib. bdg.)— ISBN 0-86505-816-4 (pbk.)
1. Afro-American authors—20th century—Biography—Juvenile literature. 2. Afro Americans in literature—Juvenile literature. [1. Authors, American. 2. Afro-Americans—Biography.] I. Title. II. Series. Rediger, Pat, 1966- Outstanding African Americans series.
   PS153.N5042 1996
   810.9'896073—dc20

95-32076
CIP
AC

Contents

Maya Angelou

Personality Profile

Career: Writer and poet. Has also been an actor, scriptwriter, director, producer, songwriter, and editor.

Born: April 4, 1928, in St. Louis, Missouri, to Bailey and Vivian Johnson.

Family: Married Tosh Angelou, 1940, (divorced, 1943); married Paul du Feu, 1973, (divorced, 1981). Has one son, Guy.

Education: Attended schools in Arkansas and California, studied music, dance, and drama.

Awards: Nominated for National Book Award, 1970; Pulitzer Prize nomination, 1972; Tony Award nomination from League of New York Theaters and Producers, 1973, 1977; Woman of the Year in Communications by *Ladies' Home Journal*, 1976; Top 100 Most Influential Women, *Ladies' Home Journal*, 1983; Matrix Award, Women in Communication, 1983; North Carolina Award in Literature, 1987.

Growing Up

Maya's parents divorced when she was just three years old. Maya and her brother, Bailey, were sent by train from California to live with their grandmother. Their parents attached tags on the children's wrists which said that they were on their way to Stamps, Arkansas. If Maya and her brother got lost, they were to show the tags to someone who could help them.

Life was harsh in Stamps. Maya's grandmother owned a small grocery store, and she struggled to make ends meet. The family was constantly subjected to racism. Maya had to go to a blacks-only school and drink from a blacks-only fountain. Once, a white dentist refused to treat her toothache saying that he would rather stick his hand in a dog's mouth than in a black person's.

In 1935, when Maya was seven, she went to St. Louis, Missouri, to live with her mother. Her mother's boyfriend sexually assaulted her. After this, her mother thought Maya would be better off living with her grandmother.

Maya returned to Stamps where she worked hard at school and in the grocery store. She graduated at the top of her class in grade eight. Maya then went to live with her mother who had moved to San Francisco. Maya continued to work hard at school and won a dance and drama scholarship to California Labor School.

At age sixteen, Maya became pregnant. But she was determined to finish high school, so she kept her pregnancy a secret until after she graduated. Later that year, she gave birth to a son, Guy.

"I never expected anyone to take care of me, but in my wildest dreams and juvenile yearnings, I wanted the house with the picket fence from June Allyson movies. I knew that was yearning like one yearns to fly."

Developing Skills

Before she began writing, Maya was a successful dancer and singer and became known for her calypso and blues songs. Maya even danced and sang at the famous Purple Onion cabaret in San Francisco. She also performed in the black musical *Porgy and Bess*.

Maya became interested in writing when she was in her thirties. She moved to New York and joined the Harlem Writers Group. Every week, a group of African-American writers got together to read and listen to each others' stories. Here authors, such as James Baldwin, inspired Maya to write about her own life.

Maya is often interviewed about her many interesting experiences.

In 1962, Maya and her son moved to Ghana, Africa. In the days of slavery, many of the black slaves who were shipped to the United States came from Ghana. Maya was trying to find her roots and get a sense of her history. She worked as an editor for *The African Review* and as a writer for the *Ghanaian Times*. Maya wrote about her time in Ghana in her book *All God's Children Need Traveling Shoes*.

After three years, Maya and her son returned to America. She continued to write and, in 1970, published her first autobiography, *I Know Why the Caged Bird Sings*. It is the story of her life from a young child to age sixteen. Critics and the public loved the book.

Maya kept writing. She has published several autobiographies and books of poetry. Some of her better known works include: *Just Give Me a Cool Drink of Water 'fore I Diiie*, *And Still I Rise*, and *I Shall Not Be Moved*.

When she was forty-seven, Maya was appointed to the Bicentennial Commission by President Gerald Ford. A short time later, she was named to the Commission for International Women's Year by President Jimmy Carter. In 1993, Maya read her poem "On the Pulse of Morning" at President Bill Clinton's inauguration.

Maya is a professor of American Studies at Wake Forest University in North Carolina. She also continues to write and lecture.

Maya recited her poem, "On the Pulse of Morning" at President Bill Clinton's inauguration in 1993.

Accomplishments

1961-62 Editor of the *Arab Observer*.

1964-66 Features editor of *The African Review*.

1970 Wrote *I Know Why the Caged Bird Sings*.

1972 First black woman to have a screenplay, *Georgia, Georgia*, produced.

1974 Wrote *Gather Together in My Name*.

1976 Wrote *Singin' and Swingin' and Gettin' Merry Like Christmas*.

1979 *I Know Why the Caged Bird Sings* is made into a television movie; wrote script and music.

1981 Wrote *The Heart of a Woman*.

1986 Wrote *All God's Children Need Traveling Shoes*.

1993 Wrote "On the Pulse of Morning."

1994 Published *My Painted House, My Friendly Chicken, and Me* and *Phenomenal Woman*.

Overcoming Obstacles

Maya's early years were difficult. She felt abandoned by her parents when they sent her and her brother to live with their grandmother. Maya's grandmother was poor, and Maya had to help in her grandmother's store. Here she learned the importance of hard work. Later, Maya wrote about that time in her autobiography, *I Know Why the Caged Bird Sings.*

After she was sexually assaulted when she was eight years old, Maya barely spoke a word for almost five years. Her mother sent Maya back to live with her grandmother. Here she met Bertha Flowers, a friend of her grandmother's. Bertha loved books. She invited Maya to her house and read Maya's favorite books out loud to her. Maya loved to listen to Bertha's lovely voice. Bertha also lent Maya poetry books if she promised to read them out loud. In this way, Bertha helped Maya out of her silence.

As Maya got older, she wanted to live a life without racism and prejudice. When she was still in high school, Maya applied for a job as conductor on the San Francisco streetcars. At first, the company refused to hire her. But Maya kept going back. Finally, she got the job and became the first African-American woman conductor in San Francisco.

Although she was pregnant, Maya was determined to finish high school. When she had her son, she resolved to raise him herself. At that time, she had to work at two jobs.

Maya continued to fight against racism. She co-wrote a show called "Cabaret for Freedom" which raised money to help Dr. Martin Luther King, Jr.'s work for civil rights. She also organized meetings and joined marches to try and change unfair laws against African Americans.

Despite the obstacles in her life, Maya's spirit and determination have helped her keep a positive attitude.

Special Interests

- During the 1950s, Maya was interested in singing and dancing. She sang calypso and blues in San Francisco's Purple Onion cabaret. She also toured twenty-two countries as a cast member of *Porgy and Bess*. She taught modern dance in Rome, Paris, and Tel Aviv.
- Maya has also worked in theater and television. She has been a host and interviewer for many television specials. She has directed plays for television and the theater, and starred in the television movie *Roots*.
- Maya is interested in helping children. A children's center in London, England, has been named after her.

James Baldwin

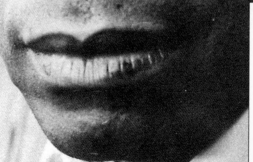

Died: December 1, 1987, in St. Paul de Vence, France.

Education: De Witt Clinton High School, New York, New York.

Awards: Eugene F. Saxton fellowship, 1945; Rosenwald fellowship, 1948; Guggenheim fellowship, 1954; National Institute of Arts and Letters grant for literature, 1956; Ford Foundation grant, 1959; George Polk Memorial Award, 1963; American Book Award nomination for *Just above My Head*, 1980; Commander of the Legion of Honor (France), 1986.

Personality Profile

Career: One of the best-known writers of the American civil rights movement.

Born: August 2, 1924, in New York, New York, to Emma Berdis Jones. David Baldwin was his stepfather.

Growing Up

Even as a youth, James wanted to be a writer. While growing up in Harlem, he spent many hours reading. He often slipped away from his parents' strict, religious home to watch plays and movies. He wanted to experience as much of life as he could. His family lived in poverty, and these activities gave him a chance to dream about a better life.

In 1938, when he was fourteen, James became a junior minister in the Pentecostal church. He preached sermons that were greatly enjoyed by the congregation, but, by the time he was eighteen, he began to question the Christian church's message for blacks. James left the ministry because he felt Christianity taught African Americans to accept their inequality.

James was an excellent student who earned the support of his teachers. But he had no chance of going to college. His family had very little money, and James had to get a job. He worked as a handyman, waiter, dishwasher, as well as in a defense factory. But James wanted to be a writer. He moved to Greenwich Village, an area of New York City noted for its writers and artists. He began writing a novel and articles for magazines and newspapers while supporting himself with odd jobs.

"As they [his brothers and sisters] were born, I took them over with one hand and held a book with the other...in this way...I read just about everything I could get my hands on."

James read books and wrote whenever he had the chance.

Developing Skills

James's big break happened when he met the well-known novelist Richard Wright. He was James's hero, and the two became friends. Richard helped James get a fellowship which gave him money to write and take university classes. Soon James's articles appeared in well-respected magazines such as *Nation*, *New Leader*, and *Commentary*. In 1948, James was given another fellowship and used the money to travel to France.

In Paris, James began to write full time. He quickly finished his first novel, *Go Tell It on the Mountain*. This book was based partly on James's own experiences. It is the story of a teenaged boy who struggles with a strict stepfather. Soon after, James wrote a play, *The Amen Corner*, which was inspired by his years with the Pentecostal church.

In his thirties, James gave many speeches about the civil rights movement.

While in France, James continued to write articles for some of America's most important magazines. Most of his writing focussed on the living conditions of African Americans just before the civil rights movement.

In his early thirties, James returned to the United States where he stayed until he was almost fifty. He was soon in demand as a public speaker. During the civil rights period, he warned whites that their unfair treatment of African Americans would result in black anger and violence.

Few people listened to James, and violence broke out in several American cities. Three of his close friends — Medgar Evers, Martin Luther King, Jr., and Black Muslim leader Malcolm X — were assassinated. All three were civil rights leaders. James was saddened by life in America. He felt the differences between blacks and whites could not be settled. He decided his speeches and essays could not change the way African Americans were treated.

James in 1963 writing in his New York apartment.

At age forty-eight, James moved to France permanently but remained an American citizen all his life. He thought of himself as a commuter between two countries. He continued to write, but his books were no longer just about black people and their problems. He died in 1987 and was buried in a Harlem cemetery. Hundreds of writers, politicians, and entertainers attended his funeral.

Accomplishments

1946 Articles first appeared in such respected journals as *Nation, New Leader*, and *Commentary*.

1953 Completed first novel, *Go Tell It on the Mountain*.

1955 Wrote first play, *The Amen Corner*.

1963 Completed the highly regarded essay *The Fire Next Time*.

1985 Completed last major book, *The Price of the Ticket: Collected Nonfiction 1948-1985*.

1986 Named Commander of the Legion of Honor by the French government.

Overcoming Obstacles

Harlem during the 1930s and 1940s was a difficult place for a young person to be raised. The streets were filled with crime. James managed to avoid a life of crime because of his strict home life. His stepfather was a stern, evangelical preacher. He showed little love for James and often told him he was ugly and stupid. He often left the care of his nine children to James.

James was a professor at Bowling Green State University in Bowling Green, Ohio, in 1979.

By the time James finished high school, his stepfather had become mentally unstable. The years of struggling to feed his family had taken their toll, and James's stepfather could no longer take care of them. The family had very little money, so James had to go to work to support them. In the factory he faced racism and was not allowed the same rights as white workers. James learned how it felt to be treated unfairly. Later, he wrote about this in his books.

"I was a shoeshine boy who had never been to college...I still remember how deeply I was hurt [when the black newspapers laughed at me for wanting to become a writer]."

Some African Americans criticized James after he became a popular writer. Members of the Black Arts Movement wanted him to become a member. James refused, saying he wanted to be an American writer, not a black writer. Eldridge Cleaver, a member of the movement and author of *Soul on Ice*, accused James of hating blacks. James answered that he wanted whites to understand how African Americans lived. He felt racism would hurt both blacks and whites.

In 1986, James developed stomach cancer. He had an operation, but it did not cure him. During his illness, he hoped to finish a book about his friend Martin Luther King, Jr., but James died before he was able to complete it.

James at a café in Saint Paul de Vence, France, where he moved at age forty-eight and remained until his death in 1987.

Special Interests

- James was a preacher at the Fireside Pentecostal Church in Harlem from age fourteen to seventeen.
- James was involved in the anti-nuclear movement and was active on the National Committee for a Sane Nuclear Policy.
- James always said that he had wanted to own a sixteen-millimeter camera and make experimental movies.

Ralph Ellison

Personality Profile

Career: Lecturer and writer.

Born: March 1, 1914, in Oklahoma City, Oklahoma, to Lewis and Ida Ellison.

Died: April 16, 1994, in Harlem, New York.

Family: Married Fanny McConnell, 1946.

Education: Tuskegee Institute, 1933 to 1936.

Awards: Rosenwald grant, 1945; National Book Award and National Newspaper Publishers' Russwurm Award for *The Invisible Man*, 1953; Certificate of Award, *Chicago Defender*, 1953; Rockefeller Foundation award, 1954; Prix de Rome fellowships, American Academy of Arts and Letters, 1955 and 1956; *Invisible Man* selected as the most distinguished postwar American novel and Ralph as the sixth most influential novelist by the *New York Herald Tribune Book Week*, 1965; recipient of award honoring well-known Oklahomans in the arts, 1966; Medal of Freedom, 1969; Chevalier de l'Ordre des Arts et Lettres (France), 1970; Ralph Ellison Public Library, Oklahoma City, named in his honor, 1975; National Medal of Arts, 1985; honorary degrees from fourteen universities and colleges.

Growing Up

R alph was fortunate to grow up in Oklahoma City, Oklahoma. Slavery never existed in this state, so relations between blacks and whites were better than in some parts of the country. In 1917, Ralph's father, a construction worker, was killed in an accident when Ralph was only three. His mother worked as a maid and building caretaker.

Even as a child, Ralph developed many cultural interests. His mother would bring home magazines and opera records which her employers no longer wanted. Ralph was also fascinated with jazz and became friends with some of Oklahoma City's jazz musicians. Ralph and several of his schoolmates formed a society called The Renaissance Men. They hoped to overcome racial barriers through the study of art and thought.

In 1933, Ralph enrolled at Tuskegee Institute in Alabama as a music major. He didn't have enough money to take the train, so he hopped on a freight car.

In the summer of 1936, Ralph traveled north to New York City in search of work. He needed to earn enough money to pay for his last year of college.

Ralph believed that racism and prejudice could be overcome through art and literature.

Developing Skills

R alph settled in Harlem, but he could not find a job that would pay enough to let him save for college. He worked as a waiter and freelance photographer and studied sculpture in his spare time. Often he slept on a park bench. One day, Ralph met the writer Richard Wright at a newspaper office. They began a discussion about literature, and Richard asked him to write a book review for his magazine. Ralph did, and the review was published — it was the first time he had anything published.

In 1953, Ralph won the National Book Award for his novel The Invisible Man.

From 1938 to 1944, Ralph wrote many short stories and essays which appeared in the magazines *New Masses* and *Negro Quarterly*. He worked as a writer and researcher for the Federal Writers' Project and later as an editor for *Negro Quarterly*.

During World War II, Ralph served with the U.S. Merchant Marine for three years. He worked as a cook on a ship taking supplies across the Atlantic Ocean to American troops fighting in the Battle of the Bulge. This experience gave him the idea to write a war novel. But instead of a novel, Ralph wrote a short story about a black fighter pilot's experience in a German prisoner-of-war camp. After that, he began work on *The Invisible Man*, a novel which was published in 1952.

The critics loved *The Invisible Man*, and the following year it won the National Book Award. It is the story of a young African American's struggle when people will not recognize him as a human being just because he is black. The book has been translated into fourteen languages.

After the success of *The Invisible Man*, Ralph went on a lecture tour in Europe. When he returned to the United States, he became a university professor. In 1964, he published a book of essays, *Shadow and Act*. Ralph spent more than forty years working on his second novel. He was still writing it when he died of cancer in April, 1994.

"One afternoon I wrote some words while sitting in an old barn looking out on the mountain; and these words were 'I am an invisible man.'"

Accomplishments

1942 Edited *Negro Quarterly*.	**1970** Became the Albert Schweitzer Professor in Humanities at New York University.
1952 Published *The Invisible Man*.	
1964 Published *Shadow and Act*, a collection of essays on black culture and folklore.	**1979** Became professor emeritus at NYU.
	1986 Published a second collection of essays, *Going to the Territory*.

Overcoming Obstacles

Perhaps the biggest challenge Ralph faced during his career was meeting the high hopes created by the success of his first novel. *The Invisible Man* was called a masterpiece by critics, and readers eagerly awaited Ralph's next work. Unfortunately, most of the manuscript for his second novel was destroyed in a fire at his summer home in Massachusetts. Ralph had the huge task of starting over again.

After **The Invisible Man** *was published, Ralph wrote essays and taught literature. But when he died in 1994, he was still working on his second novel.*

A few sections from the novel were published in journals such as *Quarterly Review of Literature, Massachusetts Review,* and *Noble Savage*. The story is set in the South and takes place from the early days of jazz to the civil rights movement. The main characters are Reverend Hickman, a former jazz musician, and Bliss, a light-skinned boy he adopts. Bliss later becomes Senator Sunraider, a white supremacist.

Like many writers, Ralph had to face criticism about his work. Some blacks disliked the fact that Ralph said good things about American society. They dismissed his writing because it was praised by white critics.

During the civil rights movement of the 1960s, Ralph saw his work overshadowed by more militant writers such as James Baldwin. Even though Ralph's writing was not so popular during this period, he never lost heart. He continued to urge African Americans not to use violence in their fight for equality. He believed that by doing this, they would discover the best of themselves.

In 1966, Ralph was a witness at a Senate Subcommitte hearing about racial problems in large cities.

Special Interests

- Ralph's first love was music. He studied at the Tuskegee Institute with the conductor of his hometown Oklahoma City Orchestra. He was on the board of advisors for the Institute of Jazz Society.
- Ralph was interested in sculpture and once considered it as a career.
- He was very interested in the arts. He was Vice President of the National Institute of Arts and Letters (1967), a charter member of the National Council of the Arts, a member of the Carnegie Commission of Educational Television, and a trustee of the John F. Kennedy Center for the Performing Arts.
- Ralph was a gourmet cook, a photographer, a musician, an art collector, and designed his own furniture.

Alex Haley

Personality Profile

Career: Author and lecturer.

Born: August 11, 1921, in Ithaca, New York, to Simon and Bertha Haley.

Died: February 10, 1992, in Seattle, Washington.

Family: Married Nannie Branch, 1941, (divorced, 1964); married Juliette Collins, 1964, (divorced, 1972); married Myrna Lewis, 1972. Had three children, William, Lydia, and Cynthia.

Education: Elizabeth City Teachers College, 1937 to 1939.

Awards: Honorary degrees from Simpson College, 1971, Seaton Hill University, 1974, Howard University, 1974, Williams College, 1975, Capitol University, 1975; Spingarn Medal NAACP, 1977; special Pulitzer Prize for *Roots*, 1977; Fellowship Commision Award, 1977; nominated for Black Filmmakers Hall of Fame for producing *Palmerstown U.S.A.*, 1981.

Growing Up

Alex lived in many towns as a boy because his father was a college professor who taught at different universities in the South. However, Alex's happiest memories were of Henning, Tennessee, where he spent time with his grandparents. His grandmother and great-aunts told him stories about his ancestor "Kin-tay." His ancestor had been kidnapped in Africa during the late 1700s and sold into slavery in the United States.

After graduating from high school at age fifteen, Alex attended college. In 1939, he joined the U.S. Coast Guard as a kitchen messboy and served in the South Pacific during World War II. During this time, he began writing. Alex's work was noticed by the Coast Guard, and they created the position of chief journalist just for him.

In 1949, Alex was the Coast Guard's chief journalist.

Alex retired from the Coast Guard twenty years later, in 1959, and tried to earn a living as a writer. It was difficult at first. He received a break when *Playboy* magazine asked him to interview Miles Davis, the famous jazz trumpeter. *Playboy* was impressed with Alex's style and asked him to interview Malcolm X, leader of the Black Muslims. Malcolm X asked Alex to help him write his autobiography. *The Autobiography of Malcolm X* was finished in 1965. It became a best-seller and sold over six million copies. Alex was now able to make a living lecturing and writing.

"At Dad's insistence, I'd learned to type in high school, and my most precious shipboard possession was my portable typewriter."

Developing Skills

Remembering his grandmother's stories, Alex began researching his family history. His publishers gave him money to work. He visited libraries, archives, and other research centers and discovered that his ancestor Kin-tay was probably a member of the Mandingo people of Gambia in West Africa.

In 1967, at age forty-six, Alex traveled to Gambia. He met a griot, a storyteller who tells the tribe's history. Alex spoke to the griot through an interpreter. The griot told him about the marriages, deaths, and other events of the tribe. He told the story of a young man named Kunta Kinte who lived in the village during the 1700s.

In search of his roots, Alex traveled to Gambia, Africa.

Kunta had gone to chop wood one day and was never seen again. Alex was stunned — this man seemed to be the same man his grandmother had described. He took out his family notes and shared them with the griot. They both concluded Kunta Kinte must be Alex's ancestor who was kidnapped and brought to America on a British slave ship.

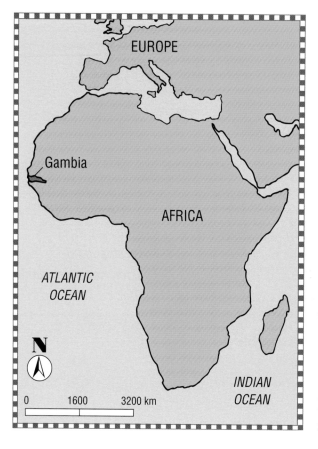

Alex decided to prove this theory. For nine years, he researched the origins of his family. He visited more than fifty libraries on three continents. In October, 1976, *Roots* was published. Critics and readers loved it. It received a special Pulitzer Prize, a National Book Award, and 300 other honors. The tremendous success made Alex a multimillionaire.

Roots had an amazing effect on American society. It was adapted for television, and more than half the country — about 130 million people — watched one of the episodes. People became interested in black history and in genealogy, the study of one's ancestors. Some whites said that although they had learned about slavery, until they read *Roots*, they had never imagined what it was like to be a slave.

Alex lectured across the country and made hundreds of appearances on radio and television programs. He spoke to an average of 6,000 people a day and made $4,000 a lecture. But the workload was enormous, and he had little time to write. Alex started to write about his father's family history. He moved from Los Angeles back home to Tennessee to get more time to write. He also continued to lecture, and it was on one of his trips that he died. He was buried in Henning, near his grandparents' home, where he got the inspiration to write *Roots*.

In 1977, Alex won a Fellowship Commission Award.

Accomplishments

1962 Began writing "Playboy Interviews" for *Playboy*.

1965 Published *The Autobiography of Malcolm X*.

1976 Published *Roots: The Saga of an American Family*.

1977 *Roots* is broadcast on television.

1979 *Roots: The Sequel* is broadcast on television.

1993 *Alex Haley's Queen: The Story of an American Family* is published after his death. David Stevens finished the writing.

Overcoming Obstacles

When Alex retired from the Coast Guard, he wanted to be a freelance writer. It was a very difficult time for him because nobody seemed interested in his articles. He lived in poverty in New York City. A friend offered him a job, but Alex was so determined to be a writer that he refused the job. After Alex hung up the phone, he looked in his cupboard. He had only two cans of sardines and eighteen cents. Fortunately, Alex sold one of his articles the next day. Afterwards, he framed the cans of sardines and the eighteen cents. They were symbols of his determination.

Alex also had to overcome writer's block, the feeling you get when you want to write something but can't think of the words. After researching all of his family's history, Alex had trouble writing it out. His publishers had already given him the money to begin the project, and they wanted to see the results. Alex was running out of time and money.

Alex on the set of **Roots II.**

"All I have to do is step over this railing and drop into the sea, and I'd be out of my misery forever. Then I heard voices – Kunta Kinte, Chicken George, and my grandmother – telling me, 'No, you must go on and finish it.'"

In desperation, Alex boarded a ship in Africa bound for the United States. He wanted to experience what Kunta Kinte must have gone through while crossing the Atlantic Ocean. Alex spent his nights in the cargo hold. He wore only his underwear and slept on a rough board, trying to imagine what it must have been like to be chained in filth. He pretended other captured slaves were screaming, praying, and dying around him.

Still, Alex could not get over his writer's block. One night, feeling very depressed, Alex climbed to the ship's railing and thought about throwing himself overboard. While he was staring into the water, he heard the voices of his ancestors calling to him and urging him to continue telling their story. Alex returned to the cargo hold, the words flowed more smoothly, and he finished his book.

Alex's book **Roots** *has been translated into more than thirty different languages.*

The tremendous success of *Roots* was a major factor in Alex's early death. He was in constant demand as a speaker and, in one year, spent 226 nights in motels across the United States. Although he wanted to write, his demanding schedule left little time to do so. All of these stresses led to the heart attack that killed him.

Special Interests

- Alex always loved the sea. He worked for the Coast Guard for twenty years. During this time he wrote a number of sea adventure stories. Even after he retired from the Coast Guard, Alex always did his most intense writing at sea — often working twelve to fourteen hours a day.
- Alex developed a strong interest in genealogy during his research for *Roots*. He founded the Kinte Foundation for the study of African-American genealogy.

Zora Neale Hurston

Personality Profile

Career: Writer, folklorist, and anthropologist.

Born: January 7, 1891, in Eatonville, Florida, to John and Lucy Hurston.

Died: January 28, 1960, in Fort Pierce, Florida.

Family: Married Herbert Sheen, 1927, (divorced, 1931); married Albert Price III, 1939, (divorced, 1943).

Education: Attended Morgan Academy; Howard University Prep School, 1918-19; Howard University, A.A., 1924; Barnard College, B.A., 1928; graduate study at Columbia University.

Awards: Guggenheim fellowship, 1936 and 1938; Litt.D. from Morgan State College, 1939; Anisfield-Wolf Book Award in Race Relations, 1943; Howard University's Distinguished Alumni Award, 1943; Bethune-Cookman College Award for Education and Human Relations.

Growing Up

Zora grew up in Eatonville, Florida, showing a bright interest in everything around her. She especially loved to sit on the shady porch of the local store where neighbors would gather to tell stories. It was here that she was first introduced to the folktales and stories of black America.

Zora's mother was a former teacher who urged her eight children to "jump at the sun" whenever they could. But Zora's father believed it was dangerous for blacks to have too much spirit, and he did not approve of Zora's liveliness. In 1900, when she was nine, her mother died, and Zora's happy childhood came to an end. Before two weeks had passed, Zora's father sent her to a school in Jacksonville, Florida. He remarried soon after.

Zora did not like her stepmother, and this caused even more problems between Zora and her father. Zora's father tried unsuccessfully to have the school adopt her.

When Zora was thirteen, she was taken from school to care for her brother's children. The next year she was on her own. For three years, she worked as a domestic servant until she landed a job as the maid of an actress in a traveling theatrical group.

The actors were like a family, and Zora spent eighteen happy months with them. But she was determined to finish her schooling. With the help of her employer, Zora left the group and enrolled at Morgan Academy in Baltimore. When she graduated in 1918 at age twenty-three, she enrolled at Howard University.

"Mama exhorted her children at every opportunity to 'jump at the sun.' We might not land on the sun, but at least we would get off the ground."

Developing Skills

In the university's atmosphere of learning Zora began to write. In 1921, she published her first story in Howard University's literary magazine. She wrote about her childhood before the death of her mother. The Hurstons had lived in Eatonville, Florida, the first self-governed black township in America. Its residents had not experienced the racism or the violence found in other towns. In her story, Zora tried to explain what it had been like to grow up in Eatonville.

Zora was the most published black female author in her time.

Zora kept writing about her Eatonville experiences, and, in 1925, one of her stories and a play won second-place prizes in the magazine *Opportunity*. Later that year, she was awarded a scholarship to Barnard College in New York City. She was the school's first black student.

In New York, Zora became involved with the Harlem Renaissance, a group of African-American writers. Using the storytelling skills that she had learned as a child, Zora brought the Eatonville people to life in her writing. Known as "Zora's stories," her tales were an immediate hit among the other writers.

At the same time she was enjoying success as a writer, Zora became interested in anthropology, the study of people and their culture. When she received her B.A. from Barnard in 1928, Zora enrolled at Columbia University to study anthropology with Franz Boas, one of the most famous anthropologists of the time.

Franz was especially interested in the study and collection of folktales and lore. Nobody had ever collected African-American folklore before, and Franz believed that Zora was the ideal person to do so.

For the next ten years, Zora researched and collected the lore and stories of African-American people. She traveled from Louisiana to Jamaica to Haiti, talking to people and learning about their culture. She found out more about the voodoo religion than any other anthropologist. The books she wrote about the folklore that she had collected were hailed by the critics.

Even today, Zora is considered by many to have been the most important collector of African-American folklore.

Accomplishments

1925 Awarded second-place prizes by *Opportunity* for a story and a play.

1934 Published the novel *Jonah's Gourd Vine*.

1935 Published *Mules and Men*, a folklore collection.

1937 Published the novel *Their Eyes Were Watching God*.

1938 Published *Tell My Horse*, her second folklore collection.

1942 Published her autobiography, *Dust Tracks on a Road*.

Overcoming Obstacles

Money troubles followed Zora through much of her life. Before she could finish high school, Zora first had to work and save enough money to support herself while she attended classes. When she graduated, she worked as a waitress and a manicurist to earn enough money to pay for her tuition at Howard University. But Zora still had trouble making ends meet. After finishing a course, she would often have to stop and work until she had saved enough money to take another.

When Zora began her graduate work at Columbia University, many people did not believe that she was the right person to collect African-American folklore. Zora proved them wrong. The African Americans whom she spoke with recognized her deep respect for their culture and accepted her as one of their people. She became more of a friend than a scholar to them, and they spoke to her of things that they would not have told a stranger.

Zora's work took its toll on her personal life. In 1927, she married musician Herbert Sheen, but the marriage lasted only three years. In 1939, she married Albert Price III, but their marriage also ended in divorce. Both marriages failed because Zora refused to give up her work and remain at home like a traditional wife.

Zora wrote her most famous novel, **Their Eyes Were Watching God,** *in only seven weeks.*

Once Zora became successful, she faced criticism of her work. Some critics said she ignored the poverty and harshness of most African-American lives. They thought that she should write about the misery caused by racism rather than about the joys of black life. This criticism followed Zora throughout her career, but she refused to be influenced by it. She continued to write about the liveliness and creativity of African-American culture.

By the late 1940s, Zora's career was coming to an end. Franz Boas had died, and Zora's books were no longer so popular. She continued to write but had trouble getting her articles published. In the 1950s, she moved to Fort Pierce, Florida, where she supported herself by working as a maid, a librarian, and a teacher. In 1959, she had a stroke and was unable to work any longer. She moved into a welfare home because she was too proud to ask her friends for help. She died in poverty and was buried in an unmarked grave.

"I have come to know by experience that work is the nearest thing to happiness that I can find."

Despite her lonely death, Zora has not been forgotten. In 1973, writer Alice Walker visited the cemetery in Fort Pierce. Here, at the approximate site of Zora's grave, Alice placed a stone marker in tribute to Zora's spirit and her work. The marker reads, "Zora Neale Hurston, A Genius of the South."

Special Interests

- Zora was interested in theater. She wrote plays and taught drama at North Carolina College for Negroes.
- Zora was fascinated with voodoo religion. Her belief and respect for this faith allowed her to witness ceremonies not shown to other anthropologists.

Toni Morrison

Personality Profile

Career: Writer and editor.

Born: February 18, 1931, in Lorain, Ohio, to George and Ramah Wofford.

Family: Married Harold Morrison, 1958, (divorced, 1964). Has two children, Harold Ford and Slade Kevin.

Education: Lorain High School; Howard University, B.A., 1953; Cornell University, M.A., 1955.

Awards: National Book Award nomination and Ohioana Book Award for *Sula*, 1975; National Book Critics Circle Award and American Academy and Institute of Arts and Letters Award for *Song of Solomon*, 1978; New York State Governor's Art Award, 1986; National Book Award nomination and National Book Critics Circle Award nomination, 1987; Pulitzer Prize for fiction and Robert F. Kennedy Award for *Beloved*, 1988; Nobel Prize, 1993; Commander in the Order of Arts and Letters, France, 1993; honorary degrees from fifteen universities.

Growing Up

T oni was raised in Lorain, Ohio, a small, steel-mill town near Lake Erie. Her family was very poor, and her father took several jobs at a time to support them. Her mother worked as a housekeeper.

As a child, Toni enjoyed listening to the stories and black folktales that her parents told. Later, these stories gave her ideas for her own writing.

When Toni went into grade one, she was the only black child and the only one who could read. During her school years, Toni began to experience racism. White, teenage boys would throw rocks at the black girls. Even though she was raised in an integrated community where blacks and whites lived together, Toni was taught at school that black people were inferior to whites.

After graduating from high school, Toni attended Howard University where she studied English. At Howard, she became an actress with the University Players and toured the South where her ancestors had been slaves. She discovered her roots and saw the places described in her parents' stories.

In 1957, Toni joined a writers' group in which all members had to bring a story. One day she could not find anything she liked. So she wrote a story about a little black girl who wanted blue eyes. She later developed this story into her first novel, *The Bluest Eye.*

"When I was in the first grade nobody thought I was inferior. I was the only black in the class and the only child who could read!"

Developing Skills

In the early 1960s, Toni became an editor with Random House, a publishing company in Syracuse. She did not know anyone in the city and often felt lonely. In the evening, she worked on her novel *The Bluest Eye*. She took it to several publishers, but they all rejected it. Finally, Holt, Rinehart and Winston agreed to publish it.

Toni moved to New York City to become a senior editor with Random House. There she helped new, black writers. She also began writing articles for several publications and was a book critic for the *New York Times*.

Through her writing, Toni explores the condition of blacks in America.

Toni published her second novel, *Sula*, in 1973. *Sula* is set in a midwestern black community and follows the story of two women from childhood to old age. Readers loved it, and the book was nominated for the 1975 National Book Award.

In 1974, Random House published *The Black Book* which Toni edited. It is a kind of scrapbook that features 300 years of black history. It contains photographs, newspaper clippings, recipes, advertisements, and much more.

In 1977, Toni published *Song of Solomon* which tells the story of a man in search of his roots. The more he learns about his past, the more he understands why he is the way he is. *Song of Solomon* won the 1978 National Book Critics Circle Award for fiction.

In 1981, Toni published *Tar Baby* which made the *New York Times* bestseller list. *Tar Baby* is the story of a black model and her boyfriend. The book made Toni very popular, and *Newsweek* magazine wrote a cover story on her.

Toni's most recent novel, *Jazz*, was published in 1992. The story deals with the history of an African-American family. Critics called it a masterpiece, and *Jazz* became a best-seller.

Toni has also written plays and lectured at several universities including Princeton where she has taught African-American studies. All during this time, she kept her job as editor at Random House. In 1993, Toni won the Nobel Prize for literature, one of the most important literary awards in the world. She is the first African-American woman to win this prize.

In 1993, Toni was awarded the medal of Commander in the French Order of Arts and Letters.

Accomplishments

1970 Published *The Bluest Eye*.	**1981** Published *Tar Baby*.
1973 Published *Sula*.	**1986** Produced the play *Dreaming Emmett*.
1974 Edited *The Black Book*.	**1987** Published *Beloved*.
1977 Published *Song of Solomon*.	**1992** Published *Jazz*.
1980 Appointed to the National Council on the Arts by President Carter.	**1993** Won the Nobel Prize for literature.

Overcoming Obstacles

hile attending Howard University, Toni met Harold Morrison, an architecture student from Jamaica. They married and had two boys, Harold and Slade. Because of their different backgrounds, the marriage did not last, and after six years they divorced.

"People used to say, how come you do so many things? It never appeared to me that I was doing very much of anything; really, everything I did was always about one thing, which is books."

Toni faced the many challenges of being a single parent. She spent her days working as an editor, while her evenings were taken up with household tasks. The only time she could write was when her sons had gone to bed. It was a difficult time, but she managed to finish her first novel when her children were still young. It was rejected by many publishers until Holt, Rinehart and Winston finally accepted it.

In 1987, at age fifty-six, Toni published the novel *Beloved*, a true story of a slave who escaped from Kentucky to Ohio. About to be captured and returned to her owners, the slave killed her child in order to save her from the same fate.

Many critics said *Beloved* was a masterpiece. But it did not receive a National Book Award or a National Book Critics Circle Award. This angered many African-American writers and critics who felt the book should have won. Forty-eight of them signed a letter of protest which was published in the *New York Times Book Review* in 1988. The letter seemed to have worked because, later that year, *Beloved* received a Pulitzer Prize.

Toni plans out her books in her mind before she begins to write.

Despite all her success, Toni still sometimes finds it difficult to write. She plans her books in her mind and writes them only when she feels the story is ready. Toni once told an interviewer that she rewrites "all the way to the printer."

Special Interests

- Toni was interested in acting and accompanied the Howard University Players, a student-faculty group, on a tour of the southern states.
- She is fascinated by lore, magic, and myth, all of which often find a place in her novels.
- Toni promotes the work of other black writers by teaching courses on African-American literature.

Alice Walker

Personality Profile

Career: Poet and novelist.

Born: February 9, 1944, in Eatonton, Georgia, to Willie Lee and Minnie Walker.

Family: Married Melvyn Leventhal, 1967, (divorced, 1976). Has a daughter, Rebecca Grant.

Education: Spelman College, 1961-63; Sarah Lawrence College, B.A., 1965.

Awards: Bread Loaf Writer's Conference, scholar, 1966; *American Scholar* essay contest, 1967; Merrill writing fellowship, 1967; McDowell Colony fellowship, 1967, 1977-78; National Endowment for the Arts grants, 1969 and 1977; Radcliffe Institute fellowship, 1971-73; National Book Award nomination, 1973; Lillian Smith Award, Southern Regional Council, 1973; Guggenheim Award, 1977-78; National Book Critics Circle Award nomination, 1982; Pulitzer Prize and American Book Award for *The Color Purple*, 1983; D.H.L., University of Massachusetts, 1983; O. Henry Award,1986.

Growing Up

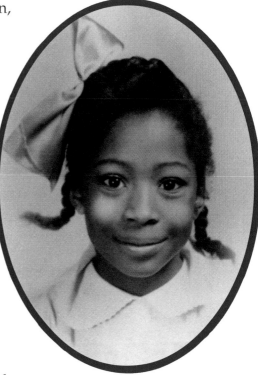

Alice was raised on a farm near Eatonton, Georgia. She was the daughter of sharecroppers — people who worked on other people's land and were paid a share of the crop. Usually, the workers were former slaves. It was backbreaking work, but her father managed to support his large family on a mere $300 a year. Her mother worked as a maid from sunrise until sunset.

Alice was the youngest of eight children. Since there were ten people living in three rooms, Alice would wander into the fields whenever she needed quiet. Books became an important part of her life because they allowed her to escape into a better world.

In 1961, after graduating with honors from high school, Alice enrolled at Spelman College in Atlanta, Georgia. But she did not have enough money to get there. Her neighbors took a collection for her and raised $75 for the bus ticket. While at Spelman, Alice became involved in the civil rights movement. After her second year, she enrolled at Sarah Lawrence College in Bronxville, New York. She was one of only six African-American students. A year later, she went to Africa for the summer. She wrote about some of her African experiences in her first poetry book, *Once*.

"I grew up believing that there was nothing, literally nothing, my mother couldn't do once she set her mind to it."

In 1965, at age twenty-one, Alice graduated from college. She found a job in New York City's Welfare Department. In 1966, she went to Mississippi to work for the civil rights movement. Here she met and married Melvyn Leventhal, a white, civil rights lawyer.

Developing Skills

While in Mississippi during the late 1960s, Alice began writing a novel. Three days before the birth of her daughter, she finished her first novel, *The Third Life of Grange Copeland.* It was published in 1969 to mixed reviews. In 1973, a book of Alice's short stories, *In Love and Trouble,* and a book of poetry, *Revolutionary Petunias and Other Poems,* were published.

Alice left Mississippi in 1974 to become an editor at *Ms* magazine in New York City. In 1977, she became an associate professor of English at Yale University.

Alice produced her second novel, *Meridian,* at age thirty-two. Three years later she released another book of poetry, *Good Night, Willie Lee, I'll See You in the Morning.* The title came from her mother's last words to her husband before she died.

Alice wrote her first novel at the McDowell Colony, a writer's retreat.

In 1978, Alice bought a small cabin in the California mountains where she went to write. Four years later, she published her most successful novel, *The Color Purple.* It is the story of Celie, a young, southern, black woman who is abused. It includes Celie's letters to God, her sister Nettie, and Nettie's letters to her. The novel was on the *New York Times* bestseller list for twenty-five weeks. It received the American Book Award and the Pulitzer Prize for fiction in 1983. *The Color Purple* was later made into a movie, and Alice helped as a consultant.

In 1983, at age thirty-nine, Alice published *In Search of Our Mothers' Gardens*. It is a collection of essays and articles about black women. She also published another book of poetry, *Horses Make a Landscape Look More Beautiful* (1984). Four years later, she published *To Hell with Dying*, an illustrated children's book. In 1989, she published *The Temple of My Familiar*.

In 1993, Alice appeared at a press conference to protest a U.S. ban on travel to Cuba.

Accomplishments

1968 Published her first book of poetry, *Once*.	**1982** Published her most successful novel, *The Color Purple*.
1970 Published her first novel, *The Third Life of Grange Copeland*.	**1985** *The Color Purple* is released as a movie; Alice worked as consultant.
1976 Published her second novel, *Meridian*.	**1988** Published *To Hell with Dying*, a book for young readers.
1979 Published her second book of poetry, *Goodnight, Willie Lee, I'll See You in the Morning*.	**1992** Published most recent novel, *Possessing the Secret of Joy*.

Overcoming Obstacles

When Alice was eight years old, her eye was injured in a pellet-gun accident. She was blinded in her right eye and was afraid that the left eye would go blind as well. The left eye remained unaffected, but because of the blindness and scarring in her right eye, Alice became shy and withdrawn. She felt that she was ugly. During the next few years, Alice became very quiet, but she also started to observe people carefully. She began writing poems and short stories about her feelings and observations. This writing helped pave the way for her later works. When she was fourteen, the scar tissue was removed from her eye.

Alice has turned other low points into opportunities. During her university days, Alice became very depressed after she returned from Africa. She was unhappy, pregnant, and felt her life was going nowhere.

Alice and her daughter, Rebecca, in 1980.

"[When my eye was injured] I began to really see people and things, really notice relationships and to learn to be patient enough to care about how they turned out."

During this difficult period, Alice started writing poems about her thoughts. As soon as she finished a poem, she would slide it under her teacher's door. Then she went back to her room to write another. Her teacher was so impressed with the poems that she helped Alice publish them. The collection was published with the title *Once*.

Some black reviewers often dismissed Alice's work because she married a white person. They also criticized her because she wrote about the violence and sexism in black society. When *The Color Purple* was published, it received a lot of negative criticism because it dealt with how a black man abused a black woman. However, the novel made people think about how all men treat women.

Alice's favorite hobby is gardening.

Special Interests

- During the 1960s, Alice worked for the civil rights movement in Mississippi.
- Alice supports the peace movement and has marched against nuclear weapons. She has given speeches against their production. In 1979, she was arrested for blocking the gates at a naval weapons station in California.
- Alice is active in the feminist movement. She has been an editor of *Ms* magazine and edited a book of Zora Neale Hurston's works.

Octavia Butler

Because she had few friends, Octavia spent a lot of her time alone reading.

O ctavia was a very shy child who had trouble meeting people and making friends. She was so timid that she could not give an oral report in school. Some of her teachers did not understand her problem and embarrassed Octavia in front of the class.

Because she had few friends, Octavia spent a lot of her time alone reading. She loved to daydream and began imagining wonderful stories. In 1957, when she was ten years old, she started writing down these stories and has not stopped writing since.

Some teachers noticed Octavia's writing talent. Mr. Pfaff, her grade-eight science teacher, was very helpful. He typed and corrected a story that Octavia, at thirteen, wanted to submit to a science fiction magazine.

After graduating from high school, Octavia went to college but left after a few years because she was unhappy with the creative writing courses. But she was determined to continue writing. To support herself, Octavia took on low-paying jobs and did all her writing at night. She also attended workshops for science fiction writers.

Octavia published her first novel, *Patternmaster*, in 1976. The novel was a success, and Octavia could turn to writing full-time. *Patternmaster* was the first in a series of novels which includes: *Mind of My Mind* (1977), *Survivor* (1978), *Wild Seed* (1980), and *Clay's Ark* (1984). The stories take place from the early days of Africa to the distant future. They are about a group of telepaths, or people who can read minds, who are stopped by an alien race.

Octavia published *Kindred* (1979) at age thirty-two. It is the story of a black woman who goes back in time to slave days in Maryland. The woman must save the life of a white plantation owner because he is one of her ancestors. If she does not save him, she will never be born.

Personality Profile

Career: A critically acclaimed author, she is the first African-American woman to enjoy success as a science fiction writer.

Born: June 22, 1947, in Pasadena, California, to Laurice and Octavia Butler.

Education: Pasadena City College, B.A., 1968; California State University, 1969.

Awards: Hugo Award for *Speech Sounds*, 1984; Hugo, Nebula, and Locus Awards for "Bloodchild," 1985.

In 1985, at age thirty-eight, Octavia received the top honors in science fiction writing. She received the Hugo Award, the Nebula Award, and the Locus Award for her short story "Bloodchild." It tells the story of males on another planet who bear the children of an alien race.

Octavia began another series in the late 1980s. The novels include *Dawn* (1987), *Adulthood Rites* (1988), and *Imago* (1989). The books are about the survivors of a nuclear war who are saved by an alien race known as the "Oankali."

Octavia now lives and works in Pasadena, California. Even though she writes about the future, she uses a large, old-fashioned typewriter. She is working on a new series that will focus on space exploration.

Accomplishments

1960 Octavia submitted her first article to a science fiction magazine at age thirteen.

1976 Octavia's first novel, *Patternmaster*, was published.

1979 *Kindred* was published.

1985 Octavia's short story "Bloodchild" was awarded the Hugo Award, the Nebula Award, and the Locus Award. All are top prizes for science fiction writing.

1987 Octavia published the first book in a trilogy, *Dawn. Adulthood Rites* and *Imago* followed in 1988 and 1989.

Ernest Gaines

W hen their parents moved to California in search of a better life, Ernest and his five brothers and sisters were raised by their great-aunt in Louisiana. By the time Ernest was nine, he was working in the fields, digging potatoes for fifty cents a day. He could go to school only between the spring and fall work periods. Fortunately, Ernest was a fast learner, and soon he was reading the newspaper to the rest of the family.

Ernest's great-aunt Augusteen was the greatest influence in his life. She had no legs and had to crawl on the floor to get around. But she still did everything to take care of the children. She cooked, washed the clothes, and even tended the vegetable garden. From her, Ernest learned courage and discipline.

Fortunately, Ernest was a fast learner, and soon he was reading the newspaper to the rest of the family.

In 1948, when he was fifteen, Ernest's parents had earned enough money to send for him, and he was able to leave the South. He went to live in Vallejo, California, where he was able get a better education than in Louisiana. Here the public libraries were open to blacks, whereas in Louisiana they were not. Ernest became especially interested in reading, usually about life in the South. But he found that many of these books did not describe the hardships that blacks faced. By 1950, when he was seventeen years old and still at school, Ernest was writing these stories.

He first began to write by hand but finally convinced his mother to rent a typewriter for him. He spent twelve hours a day typing his first novel on book-sized pages. Ernest thought the publisher would simply bind the pages together into a book. He was quite depressed when the publisher returned his pages. Luckily, Ernest was not discouraged from future writing.

By 1957, Ernest's short stories began to appear regularly in *Transfer*, a small San Francisco magazine. He won a fellowship to Stanford University to study creative writing. Here he continued to write short stories and began reworking *Catherine Carmier,* the novel he had started in high school. The book was published in 1964, followed by *Of Love and Dust* (1967) and a book of short stories titled *Bloodline* (1968).

In 1968, Ernest began working on what was to be his masterpiece, *The Autobiography of Miss Jane Pittman*. He went home to Louisiana to research the story and spent hours in the Louisiana State University Library, looking at photographs from the days of slavery. He interviewed many black people and taped their conversations and memories. The end result was *The Autobiography of Miss Jane Pittman* which was published in 1971. The storyteller in the book is a courageous 101-year-old woman — a character based on his great-aunt Augusteen. It takes place from the time she was born into slavery until she dies during the civil rights movement of the 1960s.

The Autobiography of Miss Jane Pittman became a voice for many blacks who suffered through those times but were unable to record their hardships. The book was adapted for television in 1974 and won nine Emmy awards.

Ernest continued to write, publishing *In My Father's House* in 1978, *A Gathering of Old Men* in 1983, and *A Lesson before Dying* in 1993.

Accomplishments

1956 First short stories appeared in *Transfer*.	**1971** Published *The Autobiography of Miss Jane Pittman*.
1964 Published *Catherine Carmier*.	**1978** Published *In My Father's House*.
1967 Published *Of Love and Dust*.	**1983** Published *A Gathering of Old Men*.
1968 Published *Bloodline*, a book of short stories.	**1993** Published *A Lesson before Dying*.
1971 Published *A Long Day in November*, originally a story in *Bloodline*.	

Nikki Giovanni

R ebellion runs in Nikki's family. Her grandmother did not believe blacks were inferior and often talked back if she was insulted by a white person. The rest of her family were afraid she would be killed for her beliefs, so they snuck her out of Albany, Georgia, in the middle of the night. Nikki's grandparents settled in Knoxville, Tennessee, the first large town they reached.

Nikki inherited her grandmother's personality. Nikki went to Fisk University, a black university in Nashville and ran into trouble with the administration. During a Thanksgiving weekend, Nikki wanted to return to her grandparents' home. Her grandfather was sick, and her grandmother needed her help. She left Fisk without the approval of the dean of women and was expelled. Nikki felt that staying with her grandparents was more important than obeying the rules of Fisk.

She later returned to Fisk and received a B.A. degree with honors in history in 1967. She also became a supporter of the civil rights movement and was a founding member of the university's Student Nonviolent Coordinating Committee (SNCC). The group worked for equal treatment for African Americans but did not support violence.

Nikki's first poetry book, *Black Feeling, Black Talk*, was published in the mid-1960s. *Black Judgement* was published in 1968. Both books examined the need for a sharp change in the way blacks were treated and how they should regard themselves. Soon Nikki became known as the "Princess of Black Poetry."

Nikki was twenty-six when she gave birth to her son, Thomas Watson, in 1969. She wanted to provide him with positive images of the things African Americans have done. So Nikki established her own company, Niktom Limited, to publish books especially for African Americans.

During the 1970s, Nikki produced several volumes of poetry. She published *My House* (1972), *The Women and the Men* (1975), and *Cotton Candy on a Rainy Day* (1978). In these poems she wrote about herself and her relationships with people. They celebrated the strong aspects of black life and encouraged people to make the world a better place.

In 1971, Nikki produced a record album of her poems. Her album, *Truth Is on Its Way*, became the best-selling spoken album of the year. It helped Nikki begin a new career as a public speaker and reader of her own poetry.

Personality Profile

Career: Poet, professor, publisher, and speaker. Her poems reflect her pride in black heritage.

Born: June 7, 1943, in Knoxville, Tennessee, to Jones and Yolande Giovanni.

Education: Fisk University, B.A. with honors, 1967.

Awards: Grant from the Ford Foundation, 1967; National Endowment for the Arts, 1968; American Library Association Award, 1973; Woman of the Year, Cincinnati YWCA, 1983; honorary degrees from many universities.

Nikki's writing changed in the 1980s. Her poems stressed respect for all people and the environment. Nikki's early poems were about her anger at being considered a second-class citizen. Now she felt that anger did not solve anything. It was time for people of all cultures to work together to find solutions to world problems.

Nikki has been a professor at many American colleges. She is also a columnist for *The New York Times, Encore,* and *World Wide News*. Nikki's work has been published in several magazines including: *Negro Digest, Black World, Ebony, Essence, Journal of Black Poetry,* and *Newsday*. She has also appeared on National Public Radio, the Cable News Network (CNN), the Black Entertainment Network, and Worldnet. She is presently an English professor at Virginia Polytechnic Institute & State University in Blacksburg, Virginia.

Nikki is in great demand as a speaker and reader of poetry. She also spends lots of time with young people. Nikki tells young writers to jump in and start writing because sometimes the best writing comes through seeing our mistakes.

Accomplishments

1968 Published *Black Judgement.*

1970 Formed her own publishing company, published *Spin a Soft Black Song*, her first children's book.

1972 Recorded *Truth Is on Its Way*, published *My House.*

1986 The film *Spirit to Spirit: The Poetry of Nikki Giovanni* is shown on PBS television.

1988 Two awards were named in Nikki's honor. The McDonald's Literary Achievement Awards presents a poetry award in her name each year. The Nikki Giovanni Award for young African-American storytellers is sponsored by the National Festival of Storytelling.

Dudley Randall

D udley's parents were an important influence in his life. They were both well educated, and they encouraged Dudley's interests in many things. They took him to hear black civil rights speakers and praised his interest in black politics.

Dudley wrote his first poem in 1918, when he was only four years old. When he was thirteen, he won first prize for a sonnet he submitted to the *Detroit Free Press*. At age sixteen, he finished high school near the top of his class. Dudley went to work at a steel factory in Detroit for five years. It was a very boring job, but it gave him a chance to think. In the evenings, he attended poetry readings and continued to write his own poems. Dudley served in the U.S. Army in the South Pacific in World War II.

Dudley wrote his first poem in 1918, when he was only four years old.

After the war ended, he entered Wayne State University in Michigan. To help pay for his schooling Dudley took a job at the Post Office. During his first year at university, he won an award for his writing. When Dudley graduated, he became a librarian, his job for the next twenty-five years.

Personality Profile

Career: Publisher and poet.

Born: January 14, 1914, in Washington, D.C., to Arthur and Ada Randall.

Education: Wayne State University, B.A., 1949; University of Michigan, M.A.L.S., 1951.

Awards: Arts Award in Literature, Michigan Foundation for the Arts, 1975; Creative Artist Award in Literature, Michigan Council for the Arts, 1981; National Endowment for the Arts fellowship, 1981; First Poet Laureate of the City of Detroit, 1981.

In 1963, Martin Luther King, Jr.'s church in Birmingham was bombed by white racists. In response, Dudley started Broadside Press out of his home in his spare time. He wanted a publishing company that would support black writers and the civil rights movement. At that time, most big publishing houses did not accept black writers' works.

The first book published by Broadside Press was *Poem, Counterpoem*, a book of poetry written by Dudley and Margaret Danner, another famous black poet. One of the most popular poems was "The Ballad of Birmingham" which told of a child who was burned to death when Martin Luther King, Jr.'s church was bombed.

The next book, *For Malcolm*, a collection of poems by young African-American writers about Black Muslim leader Malcolm X, was published in 1967. Dudley released his second book of poems, *Cities Burning*, in 1968. This book explored Dudley's feelings about the militant civil rights movement and the riots of the 1960s.

Under Dudley's editorial direction, Broadside Press produced ninety small and fifty-five larger books of poetry. It published the works of some of today's best-known black poets. The firm was not built for profit, and many poets refused to accept payment for their work. Dudley often gave books to stores that could not pay their bills. Unfortunately, the company did not have enough money to keep going. In 1977, with debts mounting, Dudley was forced to sell the press to a local church. Dudley was kept on as a consultant.

Dudley was very depressed by the loss of Broadside Press. He could not write for three years. In 1981, on his seventieth birthday, he published *A Litany of Friends: New and Selected Poems*. It examined the friends who had helped him through his depression. In 1987, Dudley ended his work as a consultant for Broadside and retired.

Accomplishments

1918 At age four, Dudley wrote his first poem, "Maryland, My Maryland."

1927 Won first prize for a sonnet submitted to the *Detroit Free Press*. The prize was one dollar.

1965 Founded and managed Broadside Press, a firm dedicated to publishing the works of black writers.

1973 Published *After the Killing*.

1975 Published *Broadside Memories: Poets I Have Known*.

1981 Honored as Detroit's first poet laureate by the mayor of Detroit; Published *A Litany of Friends: New and Selected Poems*.

1984 Edited *Homage to Hoyt Fuller*.

Mildred Taylor

Mildred's father often told her about their ancestors in Mississippi, about the days of slavery, and of her people's struggle to find a better life.

M ildred's education about African Americans began at home in Toledo, Ohio. Mildred's father often told her about their ancestors in Mississippi, about the days of slavery, and of her people's struggle to find a better life. Sometimes the stories were funny, sometimes sad, but all told of the courage and dignity of black people living in the South. These stories would one day be the foundation for Mildred's own writing.

One of her teachers noticed Mildred's writing talent and submitted one of her stories in a city-wide contest. Although Mildred did not win, the encouragement she received convinced her to continue writing.

In 1962, at age nineteen, Mildred submitted her first novel, *Dark People, Dark World*, to a publisher. The publisher was very positive but wanted to shorten the novel. Mildred did not, and the novel was never published.

In 1965, Mildred received a Bachelor of Education degree from the University of Toledo. She joined the Peace Corps and spent two years in Africa, teaching children in Ethiopia. The experience gave her pride and interest in black people and culture. Mildred considered marrying and settling in Ethiopia, but she decided to return home and fight for equal rights for African Americans in the United States.

In 1968, Mildred studied journalism at the University of Colorado and helped set up a program in African-American studies at the university. She became interested in civil rights organizations and joined the Black Student Alliance. She also marched in protest against the Vietnam war.

Personality Profile

Career: Children's author.

Born: September 13, 1943, in Jackson, Mississippi, to Wilbert and Deletha Taylor.

Education: University of Toledo, B. Ed., 1965; University of Colorado, M.A., 1969.

Awards: Council on Interracial Books for Children Award, 1975; Newbery Medal, 1977; Coretta Scott King Award, 1981.

During this time, Mildred kept thinking about the stories her father had told her. In 1973, she wrote "Song of Trees," a short story about an eight-year-old girl named Cassie Logan living in Mississippi. It won the African-American category in a contest sponsored by the Council on Interracial Books for Children.

When Mildred went to New York to accept the award, she discovered that many publishers had read her story and wanted to publish it as a book. She decided to sign on with Dial Books, and, a year later, *Song of the Trees* was published. It was named "Outstanding Book of the Year" by *The New York Times*. Mildred continued to write more stories about Cassie and her family. In 1976, *Roll of Thunder, Hear My Cry*, the second novel about the Logan family, won the Newbery Medal for children's literature. Mildred also wrote *The Gold Cadillac* (1987), a book about her early days in Toledo.

Accomplishments

1974 Published *Song of the Trees.*

1974 *Song of the Trees* won Council on Interracial Books for Children Award.

1975 *Song of the Trees* named Outstanding Book of the Year by *The New York Times*.

1976 Published *Roll of Thunder, Hear My Cry* which won the Newbery Medal.

1981 Published *Let the Circle Be Unbroken.*

1987 Published *The Friendship* and *The Gold Cadillac.*

1988 Honored by the Children's Book Council.

1990 Published *Mississippi Bridge* and *The Road to Memphis.*

Richard Wright

R ichard was born in the backwoods of
Mississippi in 1908 and moved to Memphis,
Tennessee, at an early age. His father deserted
the family when Richard was only six. Since his mother
could not support Richard and his brother on her
meager salary as a housemaid and cook, the boys went
to live in an orphanage. Richard later moved in with his
grandparents who were very religious, and they
forbade Richard to read anything other than religious
books. Still he managed to sneak in magazines and
detective stories.

When Richard finally began his formal education in the
fifth grade, he did very well. He published his first story
when he was sixteen. When Richard was seventeen he
ran away to Memphis. Here he was able to get books
from a "whites only" library by forging a note which
stated, "Dear Madam: Will you please let this nigger boy
have some books?" The more he read, the more he
wanted to become a writer.

*When Richard finally began
his formal education in the
fifth grade, he did very well.
He published his first story
when he was sixteen.*

Richard's first jobs were not as a writer. Instead, he was a dishwasher, porter, and street sweeper. When he was a young man, he became a member of the Communist Party. He thought this was a way of working for racial freedom, but, over time, he realized the party did not support racial freedom, and he left it. He went to New York City to try to succeed as a writer.

Richard received his big break in 1938. He wrote a collection of four stories about his Mississippi childhood and entered them in a contest. The stories won the $500 first prize and were published as *Uncle Tom's Children*.

Richard's first novel, *Native Son*, was published in 1940. It is the story of a black youth who murders the daughter of a well-to-do white family for whom he works as a chauffeur. The book brought Richard fame and fortune and sold 200,000 copies in three weeks. It was made into a play and movie. Richard played one of the lead roles.

Personality Profile

Career: A best-selling author – the first African American to write about black life in northern cities.

Born: September 4, 1908, in Roxie, Mississippi, to Nathan and Ellen Wright.

Died: November 28, 1960, Paris, France.

Education: Smith-Robinson School.

Awards: Guggenheim fellowship, 1939; Spingarn Medal, NAACP, 1941.

Most people consider Richard's autobiography, *Black Boy* (1945), to be his greatest work. The book examines how blacks were mistreated by whites but did not fight back. Both *Native Son* and *Black Boy* were great influences on later writers such as James Baldwin and Ralph Ellison.

In 1946, the French government invited Richard to France. He went there in 1947 and stayed until his death in 1960. He wanted to escape the racism in the United States. He and his family became French citizens. It was here he wrote *The Outsider* (1953) which received wide acclaim.

Richard also began to write nonfiction and to support independence movements of new African countries. In 1953, he traveled to the Gold Coast, now called Ghana, to support the struggle for independence from Great Britain. In his book *Black Power: A Record of Reactions in a Land of Pathos* (1954) Richard discussed his ideas for black rule in Africa. But he was criticized for suggesting that newly independent countries should build up strong armies.

Richard became a celebrity in France and lectured throughout Europe. But in his last few years, he struggled with sickness and lack of money. He died of a heart attack at age fifty-two. Shortly after his death, Richard's popularity began to soar in the United States. Because of the civil rights movement many people became interested in his work. Many of his books have been reprinted and translated into other languages. In 1986, *Native Son* was adapted for television.

Accomplishments

1938 Published *Uncle Tom's Children*.

1940 Published *Native Son*, his best-known work.

1941 *Native Son* was produced as a play. Richard adapted the novel for the stage.

1941 Published *Twelve Million Black Voices: A Folk History of the Negro in the United States*.

1945 Published *Black Boy*, the first in a two-volume autobiography.

1953 Published *The Outsider*.

1954 Published *Savage Holiday* and *Black Power*.

1958 Published *The Long Dream*.

1977 *American Hunger*, the second volume of his autobiography, was published.

Index

3 4 5 6 7 8 9 0 Printed in the United States 4 3 2 1